Enjoy the [sun] and the shadows on life's journey. with warmest wishes,.

Maggie 9-11-80

Shadow Lines

Linked Haibun by
  Margaret Chula and Rich Youmans

Illustrations by
  Michael Hofmann

Katsura Press
1999

Shadow Lines
Copyright ©1999
by Katsura Press

ISBN: 0-9638551-4-X
Library of Congress No. 99-95217

Printed on acid-free paper

Katsura Press
P.O. Box 275
Lake Oswego, OR 97034

With gratitude to
John Hall
and
Christopher Herold
for their editorial contributions

Linked Verse and *Haibun*

Japanese have been composing linked verse for over eight hundred years. Still very new to the Western haiku community, it has been practiced here for less than three decades. Poets struggling to grasp the intricate and highly complicated Japanese rules for linking are only now beginning to enjoy some success.

In simplest terms, linked verse is a form of collaborative poetry, usually undertaken by two or more writers. It is composed by alternating three-line and two-line stanzas. Each successive stanza both links to the one that precedes it and shifts to a new perspective or direction. Sometimes the linkage is obvious, but often it can be exceedingly subtle. Poets may link to the emotional content of a stanza, to an association, or through wordplay. There are several popular lengths of linked verse poems (most known these days as '*renku*'), but by far the most popular length is thirty-six stanzas, known as the '*kasen*' form.

To illustrate link and shift, I've included two excerpts from longer poems, both written in California by the Marin Renku Group.

first tinkling
in the downspout
now wide awake   Emile Waldteufel

on the windowsill
an empty bowl   Alex Benedict

remember my complaints?
no breakfast
and the same outfit   Fay Aoyagi

From the renku 'Vanilla Ice,' November 1, 1996

i

The rain has awakened Emile; the sound of it takes him away from his dreams. Alex notices the empty bowl on a windowsill. He translates interrupted dreams into the potential of an empty bowl. We can imagine that soon it will be filling with rain. Fay links to the emptiness of the bowl, yet turns the feeling of potential into one of frustration with a stagnating relationship.

pale winter sky—
we take off our shoes
at her open door   Ebba Story

the sunlit icicle
drips on his bald head   Evelyn Hermann

kitchen faucet
turned off tightly
old washer   Emile Waldteufel

From the renku 'Pale Winter Sky,' February 7, 1997

A couple stands at their hostess's threshold. What happens next could be in slow motion. The hostess opens the door at the exact moment a drop from an icicle falls onto the bald head of one of her guests (to her unspoken amusement, or perhaps dismay). Links? The bald head to the pale winter sky for one. For another: the door is open to the guests—the man's head is bare to the sky. It probably reflects it as well. The sun melts an icicle, just as the warmth between friends allows for fluidity of conversation. Melting can also link to the respectful taking off of shoes. Less deeply, the bald head links to unshod feet—both imply openness. The shift is from respect to humor. Superficially, the third stanza's link to the second is simply from one drip to another. Interestingly though, both the link and the shift of this stanza relate to the same emotion: humor. The shift is from good humor to ill humor.

Japanese poetic traditions have also evolved a form of prose-poetry known as *'haibun.'* It is usually composed of one or more short prose passages accompanied by haiku. The syntax is notably terse, as is typically found in travel journals. Even verbs are sometimes omitted, reducing sentences to simple phrases. Traditional Japanese haibun can range from light-hearted sketches to extended travel diaries, such as Bashô's archetypical haibun, *Oku no Hosomichi* (*Narrow Road to the Interior*).

In the West, the modernization of haibun leans away from the abbreviated travel journal format. Western writers tend towards longer, more complex sentences, and employ more descriptive language. The actual coupling of prose and haiku seems to be the one consistant commonality. In both traditional and modern haibun, the prose passages do not attempt to explain the haiku, and the haiku themselves generally link to the prose through emotional content or mood. As Makoto Ueda says, 'It is up to the reader to grasp the meaning of the prose, and then of the haiku, and to go on to discover the undercurrents of meaning common to both.'*

Christopher Herold

*Quoted in *The Haiku Handbook* by William J. Higginson, McGraw-Hill Book Co., 1985.

Beginnings

In 1994, to celebrate the 300th anniversary of Bashô's death, I taught a workshop at Portland State University entitled '*Haibun*: A Journey to the Interior Through Haiku and Prose.' Since many of the participants were unfamiliar with haibun, I introduced this form by first explaining the basic characteristics of haiku (a short, three-line poem with a seasonal reference and a surprise). I then provided a list of haiku by Japanese masters and asked them to choose one they particularly liked. This haiku was used as a springboard to write a short paragraph. The narrative could be about a memory the haiku evoked, a continuation of the haiku experience (what happens next), or any other inspiration. When the participants finished, I told them to look for a word or image that stood out in the prose and to use that to compose a final haiku. Prepare to be surprised, I told them.

I too was surprised. What I developed as a teaching tool turned out to be a very enjoyable way of writing haibun. When I submitted 'The Stick that Strikes' to *Frogpond*, the editor wanted to know what to call this form. I jokingly called it a '*haibunku*,' two haiku with prose (*bun*) in between—a kind of haiku sandwich, only the bun was on the inside. Haibun is pronounced something like 'high-*boon*' in Japanese, but most Americans would say 'high-*bun*-ku' or 'high-*bunk*-ku.' With its obvious connotations to 'buns' (hamburger and otherwise) and to 'bunk' as in 'nonsense,' I gave up trying to name it.

Rich Youmans read 'The Stick That Strikes' in *Frogpond* and wrote to me with an intriguing proposition. 'What if two poets, loosely adapting the rules of renku, created a piece of linked haibun? It could begin with your form: one poet's haiku used as a starting point, a second poet supplying a prose passage and closing haiku, then sending the whole thing back. The first poet would then write a prose passage based on the closing haiku, though taking the piece in a new direction (as in renku). A closing haiku would again be supplied and the process would repeat. It would end at a point mutually agreed upon. What do you think?'

Enclosed with Rich's letter was an opening haibun, which began with a haiku from my book *Grinding my ink*. I had been admiring his haibun in *Frogpond* and *Modern Haiku* for some time and happily responded with a prose and haiku link of my own. Thus began our collaboration.

From the onset, we agreed to keep our linking fluid, to enjoy the process and see where it took us. There would be no rules of word count or subject matter, no need to keep track of the placement of 'moon' or 'love' verses, or even seasonal restrictions as in traditional linked verses. Instead, we would focus on the primary elements of renku: linking and shifting.

Our links usually, but not always, came from a word or phrase in the capping haiku. Rich's 'distant train / where its sound fades / one star' ends a soliloquy on unfulfilled dreams. I responded by linking to the word 'star' but, instead of the stars in the sky, I shifted into a story about stars on a spelling chart. The shift was not only a change in mood, but in place, time and voice.

In his travel diary *Oku no Hosomichi*, Bashô used a combination of prose and haiku to record his pilgrimage to sacred and poetic places. By seeking out these famous landmarks, he hoped to commune with noted poets of the past. In *Shadow Lines*, landscape is not our primary impulse. Rather, it serves to set the scene as we revisit places of our past through memories and reflections. Place names (Barnegat Bay, Guèthary, Hawaii, the Himalayas) are worked into the fabric of the prose as we view them from new perspectives. But it is the people who light up the stories in *Shadow Lines*: ourselves as children, lovers, explorers, dreamers, care-takers; and friends, family and strangers whom we encounter as they pass through our lives.

We hope that you will discover yourself between these shadow lines, and that you will be inspired to find others with whom to begin writing linked haibun— linking not only with your minds but with your hearts.

Margaret Chula
Portland, Oregon
June 1999

Introduction

Imagine that on the table in front of you lies a page of linked verses composed by two poets. Imagine picking up a magnifying glass and moving in, slowly, to just one three-line stanza. To your amazement, as you get closer, the few words of the stanza don't get larger, but rather multiply into a sentence, two sentences, a paragraph. The verse itself is invisible now, absorbed into a fabric of prose. As you move the glass away, the paragraph begins to dissolve; the verse reappears.

Now put down the magnifying glass and imagine that that original stanza is a person. Until you picked up the glass, you saw this person as just another human, with certain superficial attributes. When you got closer, you were able to see into the person's past; you gained insight to a particular event that contributed to whom that person has become.

Another realization dawns: when magnified, the experience you were reading is very much like one you yourself remember having. The walls that seem to separate your lives have become thinner. You empathize.

When sufficiently recovered from these revelations, place the paragraph above the verse. It is now a haibun (haiku-prose). It is also a person, and a deeper understanding of that person. You ponder. Did the verse give rise to the paragraph, or did the paragraph produce the verse? In terms of composition, it could have happened either way. Fascinated, you repeat this process with the next poem, written by the other poet. The results are the same, except that the verse/story/person is different from the first you read.

Now you're intrigued. You pick up the magnifying glass one more time, wondering what you'll find by focusing on the space between two verses. You move closer and… What a surprise! As if by magic, new words materialize, directly from the blank space on the paper. These words aren't quite legible, but you intuit their content. They come from neither of the two poems you just read; these words are new, and they embody a peculiar blend of feelings, a harmony. All at once you get it: those illegible words are an interaction between people. They are the emotional hinge where two poems meet and part. But more importantly, where three people meet and part—three because now it is your poem too. You empathize. The walls fall away.

Most of us Westerners have an insatiable need to experiment in order to give expression to our unique voices. Over the years, a number of poets have attempted to expand the boundaries of both Japanese linked verse and haibun to suit their own cultural sensibilities. A few of these new forms have achieved some popularity, and two or three have the potential to become classics in the evolution of Western linked-verse tradition.

Shadow Lines continues this experimentation: it incorporates traditional elements of both renku and haibun, yet the poets do not adhere rigidly to those structures. Rather they maintain an open attitude toward new possibilities. Not only does *Shadow Lines* stand solidly on its own merits as a unique and entertaining work, it also indicates the potential of this new hybrid of collaborative composition. On the literary level, linked haibun offers a magic combination: the broad, creative latitudes of prose composition, the clear, defined focus of haiku, and now, the fluid, bonding characteristics of dialogue. On a more personal level, this form offers a way to remove the walls between us and, by doing so, come to deeper appreciation of what we all have in common. Together these aspects of writing and sharing produce a potent art form, one that not only entertains but educates.

When I read *Shadow Lines* for the first time, several things impressed me. The first was obvious: two fine poets attuning themselves again and again to the central emotional messages in each other's work. Invariably those messages were the very ones they chose for points of linkage. Second, the essential moods lead to altogether new circumstances or to different emotional interpretations of a common imagery. There is a keen sense of excitement in this collaboration, the excitement of people discovering themselves and each other. Another point of interest is the marked contrast between masculine and feminine writing styles. And since there is no discord or contention, this contrast is delightful, in perfect harmony. Contrast, yes, and much variety as well, but there are also recurring themes in this work: childhood, dreams, travel, old age, transition, death and transcendence. Each of these is touched upon more than once, yet always from a different perspective.

Shadow Lines begins with a haibun that expresses longing for relinquished dreams. From there we move into youthful competition spawned by insecurity. The theme of competition is picked up and transformed into cooperation and mutual joy. Goal reached, the inevitable sense of restlessness arises in the next haibun, visited through a prescient dream. The outcome of all dreams is that they end. Abruptly we are transported to a new reminiscence of insecurity, and the passing of a life. In this segment, the insecurity is transformed into an end-game played with courage and grace.

There is a saying that we must see the truth as the truth and the false as the false, and that we must also see the false in the truth, and the truth in the false. In the next haibun we are taken through all four of these perceptions. In light of this realization, appropriate action is taken by the poet (then a child) by simply allowing circumstances to be what they are. Facing reality is taken up again in the subsequent haibun, but this poet's liberation comes through taking action. Again and again we approach death and, in different ways, with different emotions, return. We are ushered from accidental injury to intentional abuse and on to natural upheavals which periodically obliterate the frivolities of humanity. We see ourselves gradually becoming our parents. We visit the desperation and vanity of aging. We attempt to escape grieving through fantasy. And finally, with the metamorphosis of a concrete visual image, the barrier between material and immaterial dissolves, fears are released, and there follows the mystical experience of transcendence.

Christopher Herold
Port Townsend, Washington
June 1999

watching the fish pond
fill up with shadows
a distant train

MC

watching the fish pond
fill up with shadows
    a distant train

It comes through the leaves of dogwood and elm: the insistent clacking of iron wheels, the bulk of train disrupting space, traveling toward a red sun. I stand on the bank and listen, alone. When I arrived this pond provided peace: the water calm, the air cool, the nearby leaves softly shushing. In the pond, minnows darted through shallow water, content with no more than what they had. And for that moment, I felt the same: satisfied with my life, the comfort of the familiar, in a town three miles from my birth. Now twilight shadows seep into the pond; the air has grown chill, and far off the dark rushing sound of a train moves toward stations unknown. I imagine the train's windows—still frames of a movie—filled with faces I will never know, in transit toward places I will never see. I think of all the sites of which I once dreamed—the canals of Venice, the pubs of London, the Eiffel Tower framing blue sky—and the dreams return, though now with an ache. The sound of the train diminishes, shadows deepen to night.

distant train
where its sound fades
one star

RY

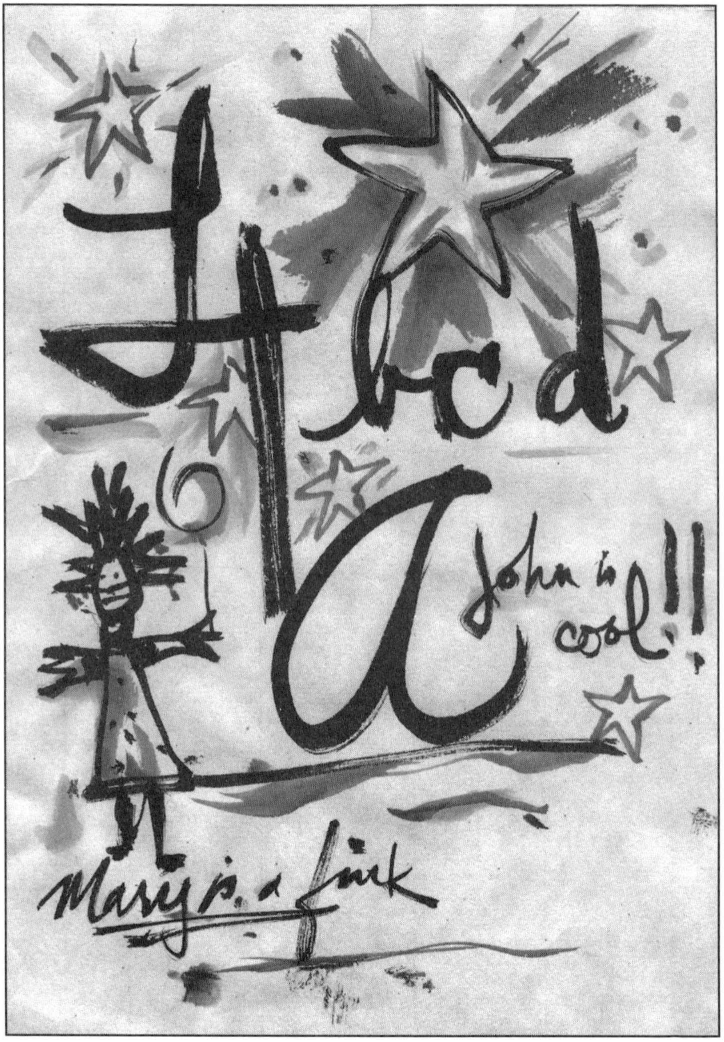
bcd
John is cool!!
Mary is a fink

One star and then another. All year I watched gold stars follow in succession, like a linear constellation, across the spelling chart. Fifth grade, Mrs. Parker's class. I was a tall, gangly girl, but I could spell. Spelling counted for a lot in those days, as did good handwriting, at least among the girls. Once a month Miss Cramer, the regional penmanship expert, would come to Northfield Elementary to grade our handwriting with a 1, 2, or 3 stamped across the top of selected homework. Susan Leonard and I were the only students who got straight 1's for excellence; we were also tied for gold stars in spelling. At the end of the year, Mrs. Parker set up a spelling bee to determine the winner. Susan didn't need to win as much as I did. She was popular and already wore a bra. Sitting behind her I was made aware of this by the thin white blouses she had taken to wearing. On the day of the spelling bee, as expected, only Susan and I were left standing. For ten minutes we kept up the volley. Finally she went down on the word 'freight.' I spelled it correctly and earned the last gold star. When I saw Susan twenty-five years later at our high school reunion, she confessed to having traced my handwriting in fifth grade. At the end of the evening, she wrote down her address in meticulous penmanship. When she asked for mine, I purposely scribbled it so it was nearly illegible.

childhood memory
this morning hen scratchings
on new snow

MC

5

New snow overnight—another six inches on top of twelve. Our lawn, our driveway, the flagstone walk, all have become a field of white; only the slender birches, ghostly and bare, provide any hint of what lies beneath. Ann and I put on our heavy boots, our woolen coats and scarves, our leather gloves; together, armed with red plastic shovels, we enter this new world. The sky still has the look of snow, and our breath plumes. Undaunted, I head toward the bottom of the driveway, where plows have built minor mountains. I begin shoveling, taking snow off layer by layer, while Ann starts on the front steps. Soon my body finds its rhythm: my arms and heart pump in unison, and the red shovel jumps like a flame. Periodically, I look at Ann as she steadily moves toward the driveway. After an hour, only a few yards separate us. Then, once more, it begins to snow: large flakes, immaculate geometries, cascading through the air. We look up at the falling sky, then I look at Ann, her small face glowing with work and joy. She looks at me; we smile, and the same thought hits. Plunging our shovels into snow, we begin a narrow path straight to each other: two flames leaping wildly, until we meet and throw our shovels aside. Embracing, we kiss in the magical air...

chapter's end
in the white space, room
for dreaming

RY

Last night I dreamed about my dream house. 'Why are we buying a house in Japan?' I ask John as we remove our shoes in the entryway. The house has many rooms, all furnished with valuable antiques. In the hallway is a cherrywood *tansu* with thin narrow drawers for storing kimonos. The former owner, a Japanese sage, collected soaps, and the tansu contains samples all carefully labeled and numbered. I open drawer after drawer, enjoying their exotic scents and the calligraphy on the wrappers. Then, getting down to more practical matters, I ask the daughter of the sage if the house has a washer and dryer. She leads me to a small room. 'Here,' she says, pointing to an empty space in the corner. I smile and nod. Looking out the window, I spy a small cottage. 'What's that?' I ask. 'I am not allowed to show you that place,' she whispers, and leaves abruptly. From the window I have a clear view into one of the cottage rooms. It is filled with Japanese dolls. As if on cue, two life-size dolls stand up and begin to dance. Then smaller ones, like dwarves at their feet, rise to join them. Hands outstretched, they twirl as if entranced. I watch the dance of the dolls for awhile, then turn away sadly.

'We cannot live here,' I say to John, and we leave the dream house. But all the next day, I find myself revisiting, one by one, all the rooms of my dream. I open the drawers of scented soap, linger at the kitchen window, and

at dusk I watch
a nameless bird settle on
a tree with no leaves

MC

at dusk I watch
a nameless bird settle on
a tree with no leaves

I stare out the window at the barren tree, its leaves hurrying down the avenue, then let the curtain fall back in place. I turn to my mother; she sleeps, unaware I am here. Outside, in the hallway, orderlies push gurneys, wheelchairs, trays of capped vials. Through one wall, I hear a TV show—some action-adventure filled with explosions, screams. None of this affects my mother; she sleeps; she's fallen somewhere deep inside herself. Her pale face lies motionless, its skin pulled tight against the skull; cords of tendons rise in her neck, and her pulse flutters weakly below her jaw. Even before this last collapse, the diabetes had taken its toll: eyesight gone, kidneys failing, left leg amputated above the knee. Now an insulin reaction has left her barely alive. One moment she's listening to her talking book—*The Seven Storey Mountain* told in deep baritone—and the next she's woozy, unfocused, falling: the world reduced to a meager ledge, and she just can't hold on. Looking at her, I recall the first time I gave her insulin. 'You need to learn, in case your father isn't here,' she said. I was ten, and scared, but I did it: 2 units Regular, 4 Lente, tapping the syringe to release air bubbles, inserting the needle into her toughened arm. Afterward I watched her constantly, waiting for the collapse I knew would occur. But every time she caught me, she just smiled and waved; if nervous, she never let on. Now she sleeps, her life fading, and I must be just as brave. I smile and wave. 'Goodbye,' I tell her. When I look outside again, the bird has flown away.

in late light
her syringe
—its thin shadow

RY

11

in late light
her syringe
—its thin shadow

Thin shadow of a doubt. I was a young girl when the news traveled far and wide that Uncle Eddie had shot a wild boar with a bow and arrow. A wild boar! When I looked up 'boar' in the encyclopedia, I could not believe that a bow and arrow could kill this enormous beast. For I had had first-hand experience with arrows; just that summer my brother had accidentally shot me in the leg with one. I had yanked it out, cleaned and bandaged the wound, and was none the worse for wear. My brothers and I begged Daddy to take us out to Uncle Eddie's till he gave in. The boar was dangling from the rafters of the old cow barn with a hook through its snout. Flies buzzed around the grizzled hair. Disgusted but fascinated, I edged closer and peered into shiny eyes that were level with my own. Then, stroking its prickly coat, I noticed traces of dried blood behind his left ear. Lifting it gently I discovered, in the shadow behind the ear, a clean bullet hole.

'That boar had me up a tree after the first arrow, but I shot the bejesus outta him till he looked like a goddamn pincushion. Squealed like a banshee that one! Hee hah!' Uncle Eddie, with his unshaven face and crooked teeth, beamed at me from across the barn. His friends hooted and slapped him on the shoulder. I smiled back and, as I walked over to join the men and boys, I knew I would never tell anyone about that bullet hole.

> not really lying
> just a good storyteller
> the buzzing flies
>
> MC

not really lying
just a good storyteller
the buzzing flies

The greenheads are biting, but Mark and I don't care. We are sitting in Mark's old garvey, in one of the coves off Barnegat Bay. We have both taken a day off from work—'The reprieve from hell,' as Mark put it—to go crabbing. We set out just after dawn. Five hours later, we have half a bushel of blue crabs. Occasionally we check a trap, but mostly we just sit, slap at the flies, and tell stories—biggest crab ever caught, most weight ever lifted, most beautiful woman ever laid—typical tall tales that neither of us believes. Sunlight falls on the water in pieces, as if the gods were throwing their own bait, and a light breeze cuts the heat.

Around noon we break out two beers and eat ham-and-cheese hoagies. Talk quiets, and sounds are few: the lapping of bay water against the hull; the incessant buzzing of flies; the clicking and scrabbling of the crabs. We finish the hoagies, open two more beers. On his third beer, Mark spreads his arms wide. 'This is the life. No alarms, no cubicles, no meaningless deadlines—just water and air and sky.' This pronouncement doesn't surprise me. A frustrated novelist, Mark now writes promotional copy for a bio-tech firm in North Jersey and hates it—particularly so during the last few months. He's constantly moaning about his cramped gray-and-blue cubicle, the growing list of deadlines and projects tacked near his monitor.

'Wouldn't it be wonderful to get a second chance?' he says, taking another sip of his beer. 'To be able to return to all those forks in our path, and take the road less traveled?' I nod. 'Yeah,' he says, 'to be able to do what you want, when you want, where you want— what a life!'

Mark takes one of the pairs of tongs and picks up a crab. 'Poor little fellow,' he says. 'Out of your element, trapped, not knowing where to turn.' He pauses,

turning the crab this way, that. 'Sometimes I know just how you feel.' With a flick of his wrist, he flings the blue crab into the bay. We both follow the arc, until the crab hits the water with a satisfying plop. Mark smiles and picks out another one. 'Yeah, wouldn't it be nice to have someone come and take us away from all those places that make us miserable—to come and set us free.' He flicks again. I'm about to reach out and take the tongs away when I stop: Mark seems so happy, and a few lost crabs won't make a difference to our dinner. I watch him gleefully toss another crab, and think of my own job, editing college textbooks. Unlike Mark, I enjoy my work: it's good and steady, if a bit humdrum, but then I've never had Mark's ambition. Still, there are days when if I have to correct one more dangling participle or deal with one more prima donna professor....

Soon Mark and I are both pitching crabs into the air, pulling them from the basket like two kids searching for a hidden prize. Plop, plop, plop.... On it goes, until the last crab has been delivered. We stare after it, until all we can see are our mirrored faces, smiling, full of ease.

lazy bay—
around our faces
the dazzle of sun

RY

It was the light, that dazzle of sunlight, that brought me up. I don't know how long I drifted beneath the water. Airless, weightless, my body lingered inside the liquid shell as waves carried me deeper and deeper, to a place of utter peace. I was drowning.

Far above, pastel lights flickered across the water's surface. I felt drawn to them and at the same time completely happy in this vast and timeless ocean. I knew, absolutely, that if I came up, I would hit my head on the surfboard. Yet, some instinct made me move toward the light.

When I reached the surface, I hit my forehead on the fin. There was no pain, only a sense of passing from one element to another. For it was not until I began to *breathe* air that realized I had missed it. Feeling light-headed, I held onto the board for support. Then, heaving my now-heavy body onto it, I began to paddle back out, away from the beach at Guèthary.

'Mag-gie, Mag-gie!' In the distance someone was calling my name. I turned my head and saw Jacques, the young Frenchman who had lent me his board, dashing back and forth along the beach.

'Look at your bikini!' he shouted. 'Look down at your bikini!'

Blood was dripping down my chest. Reluctantly, I maneuvered the surfboard toward shore. Jacques swam out and helped pull me in. Angela pressed a towel against my forehead, and we all piled into the van and drove to the nearest hospital.

A battalion of doctors gathered around the twenty-year-old American surfer girl who was covered in sand and blood. One washed my face and feet, one gave me a tetanus booster, another stitched up the wound and the last massaged my feet. Angela acted as translator.

'Your name, Mademoiselle?'

I spelled it out carefully.

'And where do you live?'

'I live in a van in the forest near Guèthary.' It was too long a story to tell. How I had spent the last of my money on a train from Paris to Barcelona to rendezvous with my boyfriend. How I had met Angela on the steps of the American Express in Barcelona where I sat crying after reading Bob's telegram: 'At Matador Hotel in Madrid. Flying to Ireland tonight. Meet me—will pay your fare.' It was impossible to get there in time and, besides, I had no money. Angela had appeared like a guardian angel. She needed to get back to her job in London and I had to return to the U.S. the following week. So we paired up—two blondes in flowing dresses hitchhiking to Paris.

Our first ride was in an air-conditioned Mercedes headed for Biarritz. Angela told me she had friends who were surfing in the nearby town of Guèthary. We could stay with them, camp in their van for a couple of days, and I could learn to surf.

'No present address then,' said the doctor filling out the form. 'How about a permanent address?'

'No permanent address,' I replied. It was true. Though I had worked in London for the summer, I would be leaving for Boston where I had neither a job nor an apartment.

The doctor shrugged. 'O.K. No charge for the American surfer girl. But you must see a doctor next week and have him take out the stitches.'

Angela and I hitched a ride to Paris the following day. The driver dropped us at the home of another one of Angela's friends, this time a former lover. 'Jean Francois will feed us steak and fine wines,' she promised. Which was good because we were both completely broke.

with tweezers
she pulls out her own stitches
—sickle moon scar

MC

Every Saturday night: a new scar, a new story. 'You should have seen it,' she says to the other teenagers gathered around her on the corner. 'Three Hill Creek punks chased us around the streets of the project, throwing rocks as big as your face. I thought we were going to die.' Or, 'Man, I got so drunk last night, I tried climbing onto the roof from my bedroom window. Fell and hit the fire escape and never knew it—I was *wasted*.' Tonight, once again, they gather on the corner steps, as the streetlight pings on and shadows creep up the row houses' brick. They all want to hear what new story she'll tell to explain the sickle scar, the railroad-track stitches, the plum-colored bruises. But Fesser knows the truth; he lives next door. Every Friday he hears her father come home from work, his whiskey-rough voice announcing his latest rage. Then shrieks, curses, the slamming of doors, the slapping of hard open palm on skin.

Late last night, as a storm flooded the streets, Fesser lay in bed and listened again to the wailing through their shared wall. After what seemed like hours, it faded, leaving only the low wind moaning its same, sad story.

cold rain—
under the iron streetlamp
hopscotch chalk faded

RY

cold rain—
under the iron streetlamp
hopscotch chalk faded

The Kona Highway runs across layers upon layers of black lava from the eruptions of Mauna Kea. This barren moonscape is the first thing tourists see when they arrive on the Big Island and it is a shock. To ease this visual monotony, people have collected chalk-white chunks of coral and arranged them along the roadside to form words, names, pictographs. A kind of organic graffiti with names of honeymooners (a heart and arrow with NEIL LOVES GINA), favorite sports (GOLF), alma maters (CCNY), memorials (IN MEMORY OF LOIS AND DAVID) with very dead flowers, and slogans like DEBBIE RULES. Driving along the highway, I am moved by the efforts people have made to leave their mark: as if the solidity of lava and coral will keep the newlyweds together; as if anyone in eons to come will care about their hobby or alma mater; as if the offspring of Lois and David will return to put flowers on their ancestors' memorial. These too will be buried under the next eruption, becoming yet another layer of history. On this island, the fire goddess Pele is queen. Temperamental, jealous, she has the power both to create and to destroy. Human-shaped lava formations are said to be remains of her unfaithful lovers. In ancient times, Hawaiians offered hogs, *ôhelo* berries and wreaths of flowers to appease her. Even King Kamehameha cut off a lock of his sacred hair, wrapped it in a *ti* leaf, and threw it into the flow of molten lava to halt the destruction of his island. Though inactive at present, Pele has been known to bring misfortune to unwary tourists who take away souvenirs of beautiful volcanic glass filaments, known as Pele's hair.

> hair from my brush
> released over lava fields
> glimpse of a mongoose

> MC

hair from my brush
released over lava fields
glimpse of a mongoose

More hair in my brush; the bald spot on my crown grows. Lines deepen at the corners of my eyes; gray pushes back at my temples. More and more, I look like...my father. His same oversized nose, his same toothy smile, his same chin with the shallow cleft. More and more, I say things he said—'Take a gander at this'—and exhibit the same expressions: the pursed lips when concentrating, the downturned mouth when annoyed. When I was a teenager, he seemed so different from me with his silver-gray hair, his rimless glasses, his laugh that ended in a giggle. I never imagined myself like him, at any age. Recently I found a baby picture of myself, cracked and sepia-toned, the plump cheeks and saucer eyes a dead giveaway. I turned it over and looked for the studio date: 1923. When I laughed, it ended in a giggle.

father's jeff
always too big
now a perfect fit

RY

Note: a jeff is a flat, brimmed cap.

father's jeff
always too big
now a perfect fit

You'd have a fit too! Just an hour before I'm to meet Leonard at the Heathman for cocktails and dinner and my tailor still hasn't finished hemming my gown. An Evelyna, specially ordered from Paris. Nordstrom didn't have it in damask rose and I just had to have that color. What's the good of a face peel if you can't show off your complexion, not to mention losing ten pounds. That week at Canyon Ranch was worth every penny. And a pretty penny it was; thank you Leonard.

The gown is gorgeous, with a Paulette neckline and Frandangles on the sleeves, each thread of fringe hand-braided—-and the Stellatoe heels match perfectly. I'm sure Leonard's going to pop the question tonight. I hope it's a Dianamond tiara. I've given him so many hints about how jewels set off my pearl-gray hair. Now if this dreadful man would only finish his job. He doesn't have a clue that my whole future is hanging on a thread.

woman in sable
an orange SALE tag
on the sole of her shoe

MC

He is sitting in the coffee shop, watching the Saturday shoppers hurry along Market Street, when his dead wife sits down across from him. She looks as she did in his memory, around the time they were married: brown hair tinged with auburn, face still shaped like an almond, only a few laugh lines showing around her hazel-green eyes. She looks at his near-empty plate: a few blackened french fries, half of a rare cheeseburger oozing blood and grease. 'You've gone back to your old ways,' she says. He shrugs, takes another sip of the steaming coffee. 'Remember we used to come here every Saturday afternoon?' he says. 'You'd always order a cottage cheese plate and iced tea, even in winter. We'd talk about what we'd do when I retired. We'd take a cruise to Alaska, buy a little summer home in Maine, pick blueberries and go fishing.' He laughs. 'Now every afternoon I just sit in this same booth.' He looks into her eyes. 'So tell me, what's it like?' She smiles, reaches over and touches his hand. 'Every afternoon, I sit here with you, watching you eat bad things and stare out a plate glass window at the world. For now, it's as close to heaven as I want.'

From the street, a passing shopper looks through the coffee shop window and sees an old man whispering into his coffee, the steam rising and, apparently, tearing his eyes.

> two years gone—
> her side of the bed
> still untouched
>
> RY

31

two years gone—
her side of the bed
still untouched

Still untouched, this part of the Himalayas where few travel. There is little here for tourists to write home about. No fabulous hotel with Tibetan carpets and swimming pool, no neo-Nepalese cuisine or classic Buddhist art. Just a hut at the base of a mountain, a trail carved by pilgrims and traders over the centuries, and the hospitality of Sherpas who have lived their lives isolated from the modern world. It has taken a week to get to Dingboche from our base in Namche Bazaar, every step by foot under the weight of our backpacks. Inside the packs are sleeping bags, clothing, and food treats such as peanut butter, chocolate, and Nebico biscuits to augment the basic Nepalese diet of *daal bhaat* (rice and lentils) that we are offered at the end of each day.

John and I decide to rest here, to acclimatize before continuing to a higher elevation. 'Rest' for John means to stay near the village, not to relax and read paperback books like other trekkers. On his topological map, he spots a nearby hill, which he calculates is about 14,000 feet. This would be a good practice run, he says. And so we head out for an early morning climb.

It takes us three hours to reach the top. John wants to explore. I am happy standing in one place looking out at the panorama—a pallid canvas of sky, mountains, snow. At this elevation, there are no boundaries, no edges where things can be given names, shapes, or colors. In the absolute silence I can hear my breathing, shallow and light. Suddenly I am filled with a profound loneliness. An ache, like hunger, an emptiness as bleak as the landscape. What would it be like to die here? My heart beats faster at the possibility. And then I see them, a flock of snow pigeons flying in formation—Escher birds that morph into black and white shapes. Back and forth they move across the blank sky, then blur into nothingness.

top of the mountain
snow, sky, the outlines of birds
I disappear

MC

Margaret Chula lived in Kyoto, Japan, for twelve years where she taught creative writing and haiku at Doshisha Women's College and Kyoto Seika University. Her book *Grinding my ink* won the Haiku Society of America's Merit Book Award, and *This Moment* received acclaim from Urasenke Tea Schools both in the U.S. and in Japan. Since moving to Portland, Oregon, she has enjoyed collaborations with artists, musicians and dancers. Her awards include first prize in the Japan Tanka Poets' Club English Tanka Contest, second prize in the Japan Airlines/*Mainichi News* Haiku Contest, and an Oregon Literary Arts Fellowship.

Rich Youmans is an editor and writer who has published his haibun, haiku, and related essays in various magazines and anthologies, including *Journey to the Interior: North American Versions of Haibun* (Tuttle, 1998) and *Wedge of Light* (Press Here, 1999). A former Jersey Shore resident, he has co-edited or edited two regional anthologies, *Under a Gull's Wing: Poetry of the Jersey Shore* (with Frank Finale) and *Shore Stories*, both put out by Down the Shore Publishing. He and his wife, Ann, currently live on Cape Cod.

Born in Oakland, California, Michael Hofmann has divided his time the past twenty years between the Bay Area and Japan. In 1972 he became the disciple of Jikihara Gyokusei, master *Nanga* painter. Besides painting, he has studied sculpture and Zen Buddhism. Michael's recent work was included in a collaborative exhibition with potters Mitsuo and Ayako Murayama at the Hakusa-Sonso garden in Kyoto. He has also illustrated poems from the *Kanginshu* and *Ryojin-hisho* translated by David Jenkins and Yasuhiko Moriguchi. This year he completed a series of *fusuma* paintings at Reigan-ji and Seitai-an temples in Kyoto.

Shadow Lines
was typeset and designed by
John Hall
in Adobe Garamond